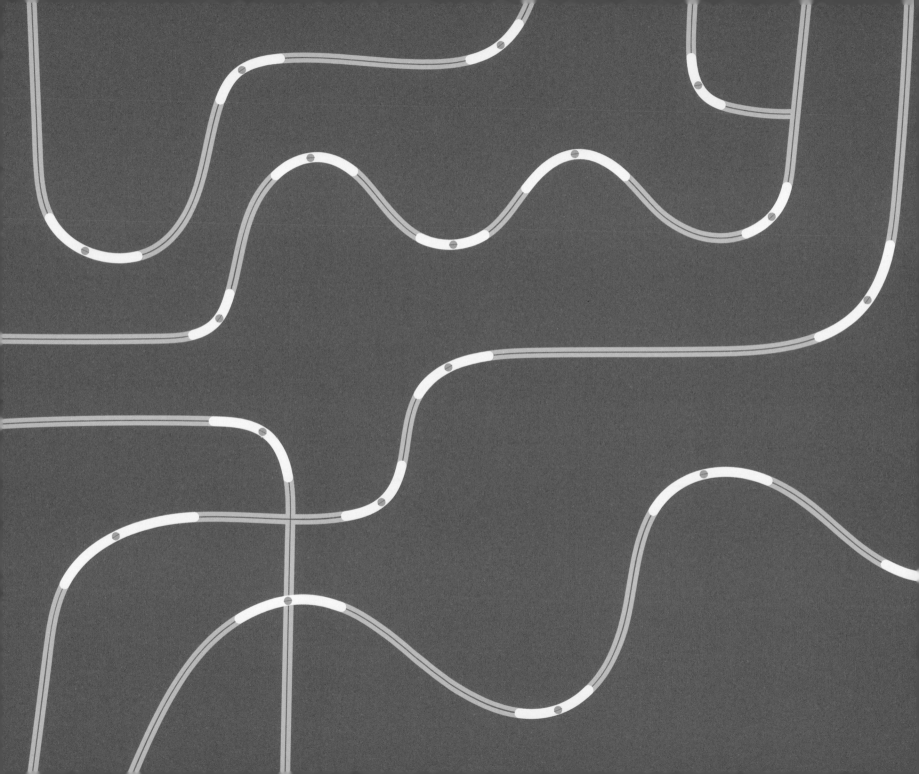

LOBE YOUR BRAIN

WHAT MATTERS ABOUT YOUR GREY MATTER

BY
LEANNE BOUCHER GILL, PhD

Magination Press · Washington, DC
American Psychological Association

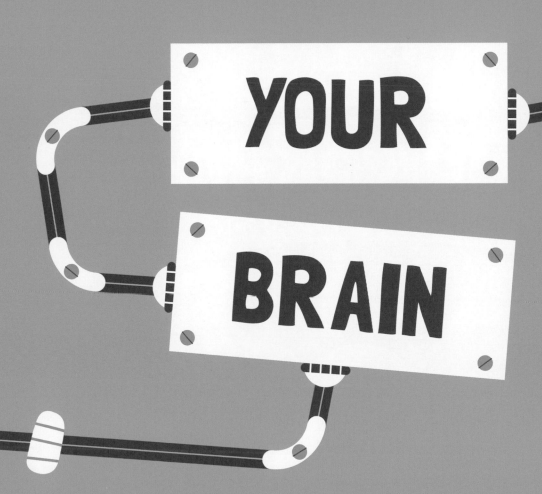

Neurons talk to one another by sending out signals from their axons to the next neuron's dendrites. For you to do anything, many neurons have to talk together. We call these lines of communication nerves. You have nerves all over your body so that the brain and body can work together.

Down the middle of your back is your spinal cord. The spinal cord is like a busy highway between the brain and the rest of the body. Your brain talks to your body and your body talks to your brain through the nerves in your spinal cord. There are nerves that come and go from the spinal cord to other parts of your body like your arms and legs.

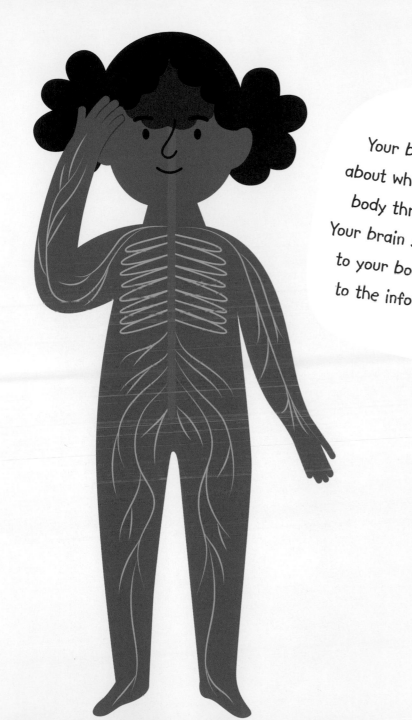

Your brain gets information about what is happening to your body through the spinal cord. Your brain sends information back to your body to move and react to the information it is getting.

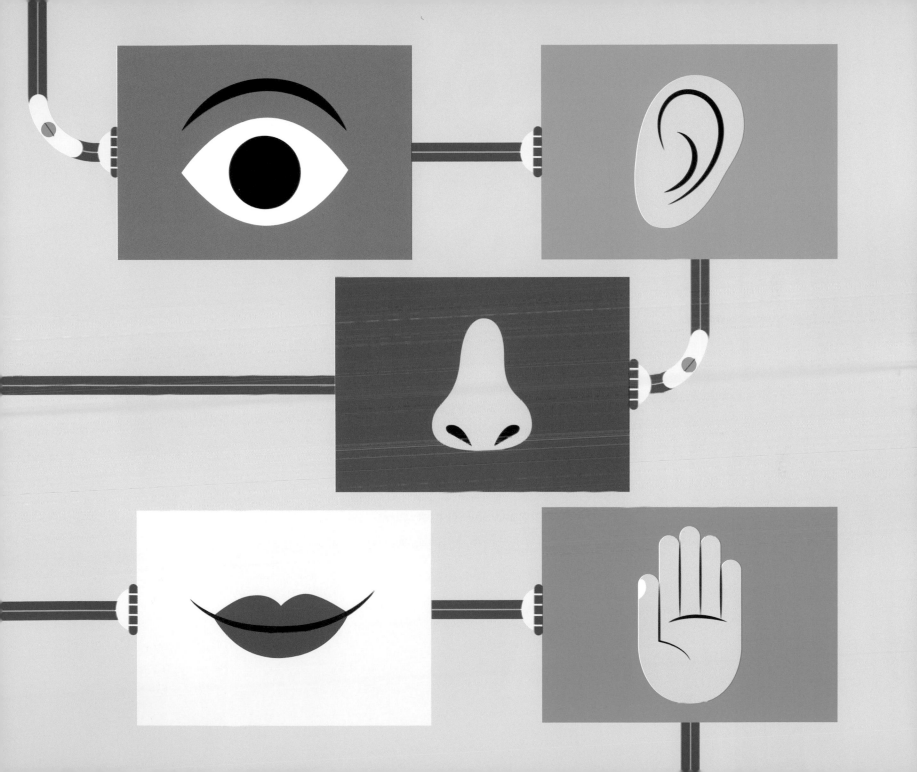

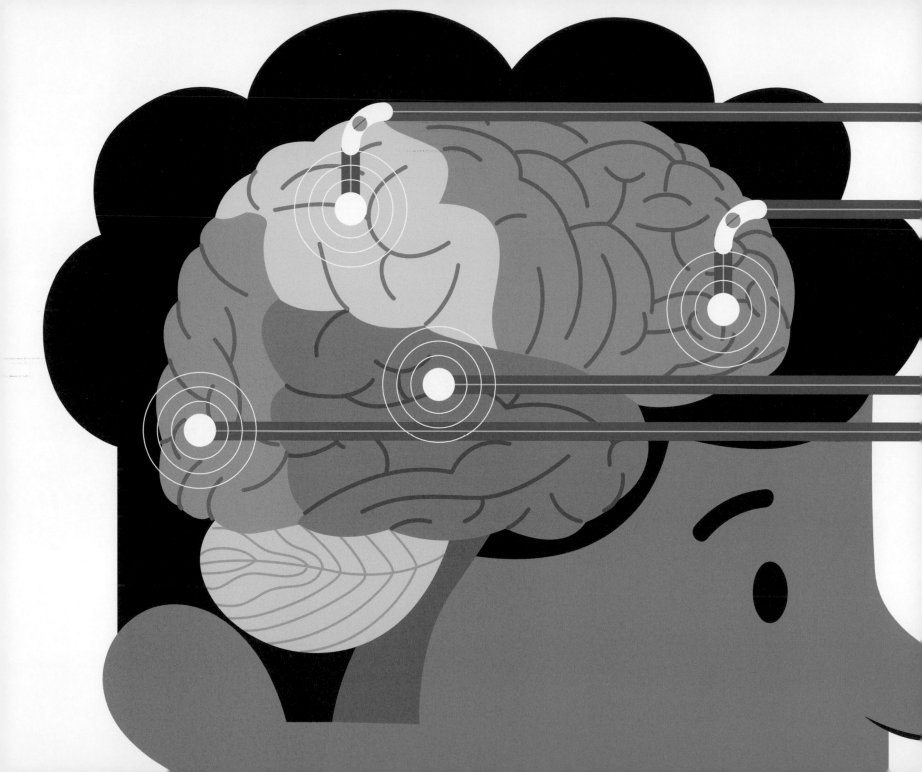

parietal lobe

frontal lobe

temporal lobe

occipital lobe

On each side of your brain there are four different sections called lobes. These lobes control all the different thoughts and behaviors that you have and do.

temporal lobe

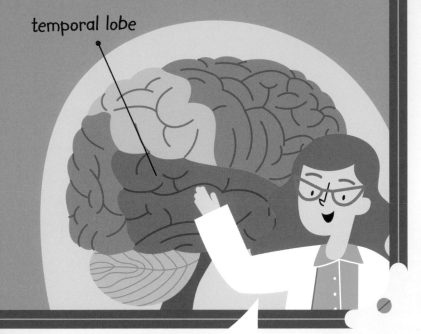

The temporal lobe is along the side and bottom part of the brain. This lobe helps people learn new facts and ideas like what your address is or what you call a dinosaur that only eats plants.

parietal lobe

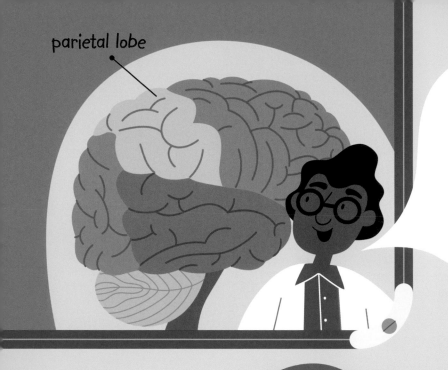

The parietal lobe is at the top of the brain. It helps to gather information from all your senses.

The parietal lobe lets you know when something touches you. It can help you figure out who is talking by matching the sound of their voice with their moving mouth.

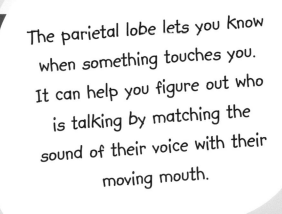

Limbic system

Part of what helps you make decisions is your ability to think about how each of these actions will make you feel right now and later. Buried inside your brain is the limbic system. This system helps you figure out how you might feel about your decisions.

While you might feel more happy playing video games right now, you might feel bad later when you step on a toy brick that you didn't put away. Your limbic system helps you figure out which feelings you'd rather have.

Leanne Boucher Gill, PhD, is a professor of psychology at Nova Southeastern University, where she received the Faculty Excellence in Teaching Award and was named the NSU STUEY Professor of the Year. She maintains an active research program studying how exercise affects the way we think. She lives in South Florida.

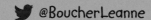 @BoucherLeanne

Magination Press is the children's book imprint of the American Psychological Association. Through APA's publications, the association shares with the world mental health expertise and psychological knowledge. Magination Press books reach young readers and their parents and caregivers to make navigating life's challenges a little easier. It's the combined power of psychology and literature that makes a Magination Press book special.

   @MaginationPress

Books for Kids From the
American Psychological Association

Magination Press is a registered trademark of the American Psychological Association.
Order books at Maginationpress.org or call 1-800-374-2721
Book design by Collaborate Agency
Printed by Sonic Media Solutions, Inc., Medford, NY
Library of Congress Cataloging-in-Publication Data
Names: Boucher Gill, Leanne, author.
Title: Lobe your brain : what matters about your grey matter /
by Leanne Boucher Gill, PhD.
Description: Washington, DC : Magination Press, 2021. | Audience: Ages 4-8 |
Audience: Grades K-1 | Summary: "A fun book about all of
the cool things your brain does"-- Provided by publisher.
Identifiers: LCCN 2020030008 (print) | LCCN 2020030009 (ebook) |
ISBN 9781433830464 (hardcover) | ISBN 9781433835155 (ebook)
Subjects: LCSH: Brain--Juvenile literature. |
Neurophysiology--Juvenile literature. | Neuropsychology--Juvenile literature.
Classification: LCC QP376 .B6915 2021 (print) | LCC QP376 (ebook) |
DDC 612.8--dc23
LC record available at https://lccn.loc.gov/2020030008
LC ebook record available at https://lccn.loc.gov/2020030009
Manufactured in the United States of America
10 9 8 7 6 5 4 3 2 1

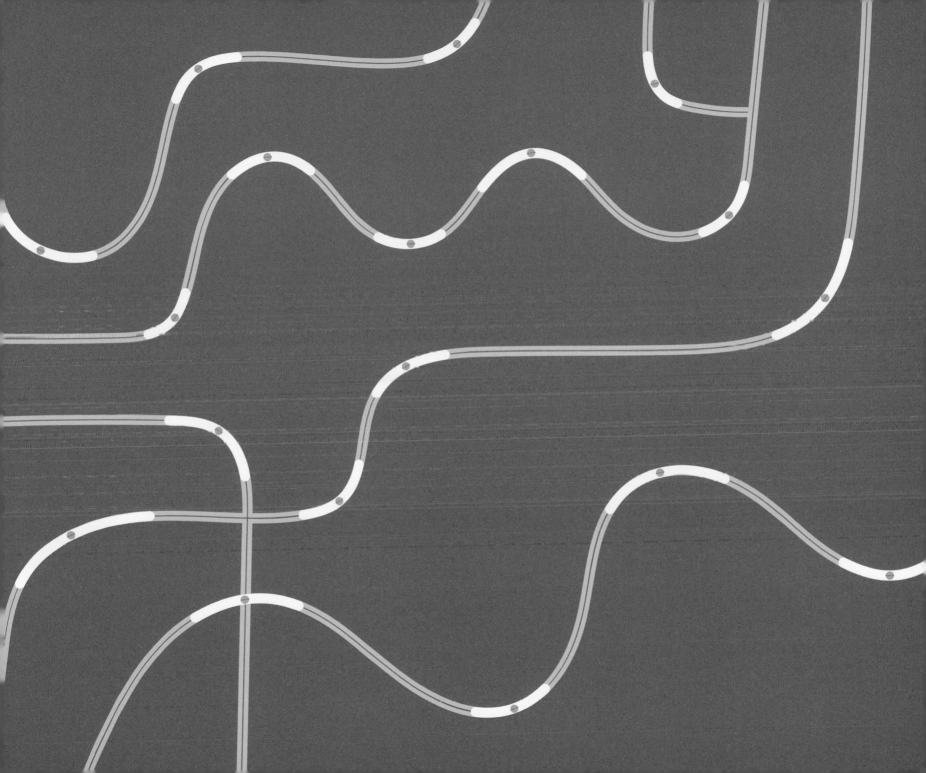

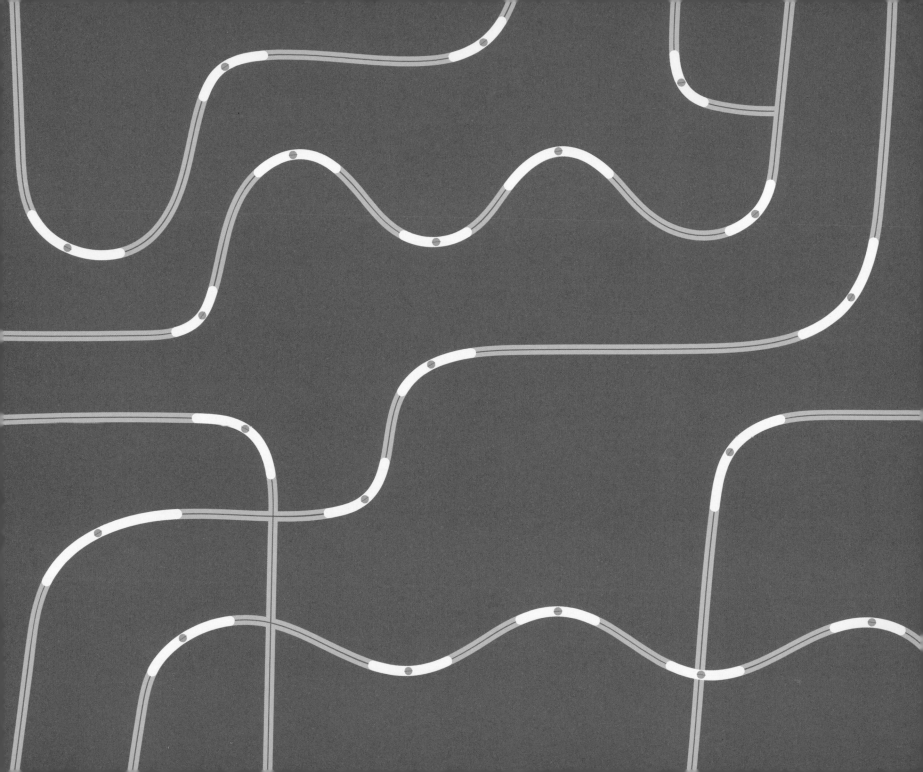